THE LONE SURVIVOR OF GAZA

PIJUSH BISWAS

Contents

A Boy Named Sami

The sun was setting over Gaza, casting long shadows across the narrow streets of Sami's neighborhood. The golden light reflected off the crumbling buildings, a mix of both history and hardship. It wasn't a beautiful sight to many, but to Sami, it was home—a place of memories, of laughter, and of a family who loved him with a depth he didn't yet fully understand.

Sami was a boy of ten, with a bright, inquisitive mind that seemed to grasp every detail of the world around him. His dark eyes sparkled with curiosity, and his hair was always a bit unruly from the constant running, climbing, and playing he did with his friends. His hands, though small, were rough from hours of soccer in the streets, each scuff and callus a mark of his youth, his energy, and his dreams.

He had the sort of smile that could light up a room. He wasn't aware of how special it was, this smile of his—full of hope and wonder, even when life around him sometimes felt heavy. When he laughed, it was a deep, genuine sound that made others laugh along with him, even if they didn't understand what was so funny. Sami could make a game out of anything, and his sense of humor was as contagious as his energy.

His family was everything to him—his mother, father, older sister Yara, and younger brother Omar. They were his universe. Sami's bond with his parents was built on love, trust, and a deep connection that was almost unspoken. His father, Amir, was a man of quiet strength. He was tall, with broad shoulders, a gentle but firm presence that made Sami feel safe, no matter what was happening outside their home. Amir worked as a teacher at the local school, though the pay was meager. He was always finding ways to make the best out of what little they had. His mother, Layla, was the heart of the family. Her laughter was soft but filled with warmth, and her touch, whether a gentle hand on his cheek or a tender kiss on the forehead, always made Sami feel loved and protected. Layla was a woman of grace, even in the face of hardship, and she carried herself with a quiet dignity that Sami often admired.

Yara, his older sister, was everything Sami aspired to be. She was sixteen, already a young woman, wise beyond her years. She was Sami's protector and confidante, the one he turned to when he couldn't understand something, whether it was the complexities of the world or the mysteries of his own emotions. Yara had a dream of becoming a doctor, a hope she spoke about often as she worked through her schoolwork, hoping one day to help people just as her father did. She was determined, fierce in her kindness, and sometimes, in Sami's eyes, seemed untouchable. Her smile always gave him comfort, especially when things seemed uncertain. And then there was Omar, his two-year-old brother, who had the sweetest laugh, a giggle that could lift anyone's spirits. Sami adored him, often playing games with him or watching over him when their parents were busy.

Their home, a small, modest apartment, was the heart of their family's world. It wasn't much, but it was theirs. The walls were filled with photographs—pictures of family outings, celebrations, and moments that made their lives feel whole. The kitchen was always bustling, with the smell of spices and homemade food filling the air. Layla would hum softly as she worked, a rhythm that Sami had grown to associate with peace. The living room had an old couch, well-worn from years of use, but it was always the place where the family gathered at the end of the day.

In the evenings, they would sit around the small table by the window, eating dinner together, and talking about their days. Sami loved these moments most—he cherished hearing his father's stories from when he was a child, stories of his adventures and mischiefs in the streets of Gaza. Amir had a way of telling stories that made even the ordinary feel extraordinary. Sami could imagine his father as a boy just like him, running around, playing soccer, dreaming of a better world. Yara would often tease him about how serious he looked when he tried to be funny, but Sami knew it was all out of love.

After dinner, they would sit together and watch the moon rise over the horizon, a quiet moment of reflection that reminded them, despite the challenges they faced, that they were a family—united and unbreakable. There was a sense of peace in these moments, one that Sami held onto tightly, for he knew that peace was often fleeting, especially in a place like Gaza, where the shadows of conflict loomed large.

At school, Sami was known as a bright and eager student, one who always asked questions and whose eyes would light up whenever he learned something new. His teacher, Ms. Lina, was an older woman who had seen much in her life. Her hair was streaked with grey, but her eyes held a spark that matched Sami's own. She loved to tell stories of the world beyond Gaza—places Sami could only dream of. She often spoke of the importance of education, telling her students that knowledge was their gateway to a better future, a future where they could help their people and their land. Sami listened intently, always fascinated by the world outside, even though he knew the borders that separated them from it.

Despite the challenges that life in Gaza brought, Sami had a remarkable ability to find joy in the smallest of things. A game of soccer with his friends, the sound of laughter filling the streets, the feel of the wind on his face as he ran barefoot through the dusty roads—it was in these simple pleasures that Sami found his peace. His friends were a constant source of happiness, their bond forged through shared experiences and the struggles of growing up in a place where uncertainty was the only certainty. They played in the streets, made up games, and talked about their dreams—dreams that seemed, at times, out of reach, but still worth believing in.

Yet, even amidst the laughter and joy, Sami's world was not without its shadows. He had learned early on that life in Gaza was fragile. There were moments of quiet unease when the distant sounds of conflict would echo in the air, when the lights would flicker, and people would look to the sky, waiting for the next strike. Sami didn't fully understand what was happening, but he could sense the fear in his parents' eyes when they tried to shield him from the reality outside their door.

Still, Sami was a child, and his mind clung to the innocence that allowed him to keep playing, and keep dreaming. He often wondered, during those moments of quiet before the storm, why things had to be so difficult. Why couldn't life just be simple, like it was in the stories his father told him? Why couldn't people just be kind to one another, and why did the sound of bombs sometimes drown out the voices of his family?

But for now, these questions remained unanswered. For now, he was just Sami—a boy with big dreams and a heart full of love. And for now, that was enough.

CHAPTER TWO

LIFE IN THE NEIGHBORHOOD

The neighborhood where Sami lived was not a place that most people would call beautiful. The streets were narrow, and the buildings, though full of life, were marked by years of wear and struggle. Cracked walls, faded paint, and rusting metal balconies were the backdrop of daily life. Yet, in its own way, it had a certain charm—a quiet, persistent vibrancy that came from the people who called it home. To Sami, it was the only world he knew, and in the midst of hardship, it was also the place where he found warmth and comfort.

As the sun rose each morning, the narrow alleys that cut through the neighborhood came to life. The sounds of vendors calling out their wares, the clatter of carts rolling over cobblestones, and the buzz of people haggling at market stalls filled the air. Sami would often wake early, drawn to the sounds of the world stirring outside. From the window of his apartment, he could see the busy street corner, where men and women gathered around wooden crates filled with fruits and vegetables, their voices mingling with the music of the radio, which played softly from the corner cafes. In these early moments, when the world seemed to be waking up with him, Sami felt a sense of possibility—a belief that perhaps today, something special might happen.

On most mornings, he would race out of the house to join his friends in the street. The pavement was rough and cracked, but it was a perfect playground for their games. No one cared about the uneven surfaces or the dust that swirled around as they ran. All that mattered was the game. Their soccer ball, well-worn and patched up with strips of old fabric, was the center of their world. They would kick it back and forth, playing with an intensity that made every pass, every goal, feel like a victory. Sami was fast on his feet, a natural with the ball, and he loved to show off his quick footwork as he danced around his friends. They would shout and laugh, sometimes arguing over whose turn it was to be goalie, but it never lasted long. Their friendship was solid, built on shared games, shared stories, and an understanding that the world outside their small circle could be harsh, but here, they were free.

Sami's best friend, Tamer, was a few years older but always played on the same team. He had a quick temper, but a heart that was just as big. Tamer often claimed he would be a famous soccer player one day, and while Sami didn't quite believe him, he admired his friend's determination. Even when the odds seemed stacked against them—whether it was the neighborhood kids from the other side of the street or the endless interruptions from grown-ups—Tamer never stopped pushing forward. Sami admired that drive, and in his own way, he mimicked it.

But Tamer was more than just a teammate—he was Sami's confidante. They talked about everything from their favorite soccer players to the mystery of what lay beyond Gaza's borders. Sami's eyes would widen with wonder when Tamer would talk about the places he had heard about in the news or from distant relatives—countries with vast forests, tall mountains, and cities filled with lights and people from every corner of the world. "One day, I'll play in the big leagues," Tamer would say, his eyes sparkling with ambition. Sami would nod, his mind racing with the possibility of what that might mean, but in the back of his mind, there was always the reminder that the outside world, the one Tamer dreamed of, was something far away—a world he would never reach.

The other boys in the neighborhood had their own dreams, too. Faris wanted to be a scientist, and sometimes, he would bring homemade gadgets or pieces of broken electronics to show Sami. He was always tinkering with something, trying to make it work again. Sami loved watching Faris's hands move with precision as he fixed things, his brow furrowed in concentration. Faris would often talk about his dreams of studying in other countries, of learning new things that could change the world, but Sami would look at his friend with a mixture of admiration and confusion. How could someone like Faris go so far from here, from their home?

But the neighborhood wasn't just a place for boys to run and play. It was a close-knit community, where everyone knew each other, for better or worse. The older women would sit on balconies, talking over the walls, gossiping about the latest news, or knitting clothes for their children. Sami's mother, Layla, would often greet the neighbors with a smile, exchanging pleasantries and checking in on the elderly or sick. Everyone knew her kindness, and she was respected in the neighborhood for her generosity. Sami's father, Amir, was equally well-liked. Though his job as a teacher was demanding, he always made time for the people around him, helping those in need, whether it was tutoring a student after school or offering advice to a neighbor.

Sami loved watching his parents interact with the community. It gave him a sense of stability, of belonging. He often felt proud when people spoke kindly of his father or smiled warmly at his mother. Their home was a place where the door was always open, where people came to share food, and stories, or simply find a moment of peace amidst the chaos that was so often a part of daily life in Gaza. Sami learned early on that while material things were scarce, community was abundant. There was always someone to help, someone to lean on, and in those moments, Sami felt that his family was part of something bigger—something that could not be measured in money or possessions, but in love and solidarity.

Sami's school, a few blocks away, was another extension of the world he knew. It was a simple building, with peeling paint on the walls and chalkboards that were often more worn than the students themselves. But within those walls, there was a spirit of hope that Sami couldn't help but catch. The teachers, though underpaid and often overstretched, were dedicated to giving the children the best education they could offer. Sami's teacher, Ms. Lina, was especially inspiring. She would often tell her students that knowledge was the one thing no one could ever take away from them. "In a world filled with uncertainty, education is your shield," she would say. "It will protect you, even when nothing else can."

It wasn't always easy to focus on studies, though, especially when the sounds of distant explosions and the presence of soldiers patrolling the streets served as constant reminders of the fragile peace they were living in. Some days, the fear in the air was palpable. But the school was a place of refuge, a place where Sami and his friends could forget if only for a few hours, the tension that hung like a heavy cloud over everything. They would sit at their small desks, listening intently as Ms. Lina read from her books, their minds hungry for the lessons that might take them away from the world outside.

But even amidst the uncertainty, Sami found a rhythm in his life—a daily routine that, despite its flaws and interruptions, brought him comfort. He would walk home from school with his friends, laughing and joking, already planning the game of soccer they would play when they got there. The laughter of the children echoed down the street, filling the air with a sense of life that was sometimes too easy to forget. For a boy like Sami, the world outside his door could seem impossibly large, and yet, there was something beautiful in its simplicity. In these moments, in the small gestures of kindness, in the shared games and dreams, Sami found a sense of peace that gave him the strength to keep going. Even when the world seemed uncertain, the neighborhood was a place where he could always return—to his friends, his family, and the simple joys of being a child.

As evening came, and the sky began to darken, the familiar call of the muezzin echoed through the neighborhood, signaling the time for evening prayers. The sounds of the streets gradually quieted as families gathered in their homes, taking a moment to reflect, to pray, and to find some peace amidst the chaos of life. Sami, his clothes dirty from a day of play, would come home to the warm embrace of his mother, the soothing presence of his father, and the laughter of Yara and Omar. It was a small, ordinary moment, but to Sami, it was everything. It was his world, and it was enough.

CHAPTER THREE

A Mother's Care and a Sister's Love

There was a quiet magic in the way Sami's mother, Layla, moved through the house. The scent of spices and warm bread seemed to follow her wherever she went, and the sound of her soft humming was a constant in their home. Sami's world was one of safety and love, and much of it was due to his mother's presence. She was not tall or imposing, but there was a grace in everything she did, whether it was preparing dinner, tending to her children, or soothing her husband, Amir, after a long day. She had a way of turning the ordinary into something extraordinary—making even the smallest moments feel significant.

Every morning, before the sun had fully risen, Layla was already awake. She would be in the kitchen, her hands expertly kneading dough, humming a lullaby under her breath. Sami loved to wake up to the sound of her voice as if the melody itself gave him a sense of security. Sometimes, when he was still sleepy, he would tiptoe into the kitchen, pulling his blanket around him, and sit at the table to watch her work. She would smile softly at him and ruffle his hair, telling him that there was no hurry for him to get up, and that he could take his time.

"Wake up slowly, Sami," she would say, her voice warm like the sun. "The world can wait for you."

It was during these quiet moments, as the sunlight began to spill through the kitchen window and cast a golden hue over the room, that Sami would feel his mother's love most acutely. It wasn't just in the food she cooked or the care she took in every task. It was in the way she made him feel as if he were the most important person in the world. Even in their small, modest home, she created an atmosphere of peace—a peace that came from knowing, deep in his heart, that his mother would always take care of him.

Sami's mother had a resilience that seemed to come from deep within her. She had lived through hardships and challenges far beyond what any child should witness, but she never let those things show in front of her children. Sami knew, even at a young age, that his mother was the rock of their family. She had learned early in life that joy could be found even in the most difficult of circumstances, and she made it her mission to share that wisdom with her children.

Despite the challenges they faced living in Gaza—where safety was never guaranteed and resources were always limited—Layla found ways to create moments of happiness. She would set the table for dinner with small, thoughtful touches: a fresh sprig of mint on top of the salad, a homemade dessert that was as simple as it was delicious, and a smile that never seemed to fade.

One of Sami's favorite memories was of the nights when his mother would tell him stories. After dinner, when the house had quieted down and the stars were beginning to dot the sky, Layla would sit on the couch and invite Sami and Yara to gather around her. The flickering light of the oil lamp would cast soft shadows on the walls, and the three of them would sit close together, the comfort of family enveloping them like a blanket.

"Tell us a story, Mama," Yara would ask, her voice full of excitement. Yara was eleven, two years older than Sami, and though she was often the more serious of the two, there was a part of her that still held onto the magic of childhood.

Layla would smile, her eyes twinkling as she began to speak. Her voice would rise and fall in a rhythm that was soothing, weaving tales of faraway lands and mystical creatures, stories that transcended the borders of Gaza and took them all to places of wonder. Sometimes, the stories were about brave heroes, and other times about animals who could speak or trees that could move. Each story, no matter how fantastical, carried with it an underlying message of hope—of resilience in the face of adversity.

Sami would sit, wide-eyed, hanging on every word. Even though he knew the stories by heart, he never grew tired of hearing them. There was something magical in the way his mother told them, a quality that made the words feel alive. Her stories always left Sami with a sense of wonder, as if the world around him was full of untold possibilities.

Sami had always looked up to his older sister, Yara. Though she was two years older, she felt like a second mother to him. Yara was smart, determined, and compassionate—qualities that inspired Sami in ways that he sometimes couldn't fully express. She had big dreams, always talking about becoming a doctor one day. Sami admired how Yara would read medical books late into the night, her glasses perched on the edge of her nose, the soft light of a lamp illuminating her determined face.

"What's it like, Yara?" Sami would ask, his eyes full of curiosity. "To be a doctor?"

Yara would smile at him, her face softening in a way that only Sami could see. She always had time for him, even when she was deep in her studies or trying to understand something difficult in her books. She would answer his questions with patience, explaining in simple terms what it meant to be a doctor, and what it took to help people heal.

"It means never giving up on someone, Sami," she would say. "It means using everything you've learned to make someone's life better, to help them when they're in pain."

Sami had always been proud of his sister. In a world that often felt unstable, Yara represented a beacon of hope—a reminder that no matter the circumstances, it was still possible to strive for something greater. She was also his closest confidante. They shared everything—secrets, dreams, fears. If there was something that weighed heavily on Sami's heart, he could always turn to Yara. She never judged him and always listened with care.

One evening, as they sat on the rooftop of their home, watching the sun dip below the horizon, Sami turned to Yara, his heart full of questions.

"Yara," he said quietly, "do you think the world will ever be different? Do you think things will ever get better?"

Yara looked at him, her expression thoughtful. She didn't answer immediately but instead placed a hand on his shoulder, offering him the comfort of her presence.

"I don't know, Sami," she said gently. "But I believe that if enough people care, if enough people fight for what's right, then maybe, just maybe, it can change."

Sami wasn't sure he understood fully what Yara meant, but he could see the fire in her eyes as she spoke, a fire that was both hopeful and determined. It was a fire that Sami wanted to carry with him. He admired his sister more than anyone else in his life, and her words filled him with a quiet strength.

As time passed, Sami began to notice how much Yara's dreams were shaping who she was becoming. She was not just his sister—she was a role model, a person he looked up to more than anyone else. When things were difficult, when the weight of the world seemed too much for even an adult to bear, Yara's strength was something Sami could always rely on.

But despite all the love and care his mother and sister gave him, Sami often found himself wondering what the future would look like for them. He would lie awake at night, staring up at the ceiling, listening to the quiet sounds of the house. He could hear his mother's soft breathing from the room next door, her steady rhythm a comfort in the darkness. He could hear Yara's quiet whispers to herself as she studied late into the night. Even in the silence, their presence filled his life with a deep sense of belonging.

His family—his mother, his father, Yara, and Omar—were his foundation. They were the ones who made him believe in goodness, in love, and in the power of human connection. They were the reason he woke up every morning with hope in his heart, despite the uncertainty of the world around them. Their love was a shield, one that wrapped around him even on the hardest days.

Layla's care, Yara's love, and their unbreakable bond as a family made Sami feel as though he could conquer anything. No matter how difficult life became, no matter the challenges they faced, he knew that as long as they had each other, they could endure.

And in those quiet, tender moments, Sami found the strength to carry on.

CHAPTER FOUR

THE SHADOWS OF CONFLICT

It was impossible for Sami to ignore the constant tension in the air. Even though his family tried to shield him from the worst of it, there were moments—brief but sharp—when the heavy weight of conflict hung in their home like a dark cloud, casting shadows over even the simplest moments of joy.

Every day felt like a dance between normalcy and uncertainty. In the morning, Sami would go to school, laughing with his friends, playing soccer in the streets, and talking about his favorite books. The world seemed full of promise and possibility, and his biggest worry was whether his soccer team would win that afternoon. But by nightfall, the ground would tremble with distant explosions, and Sami would lie in bed, trying not to listen to the terrifying sound of helicopters flying overhead, their thrum so deep and ominous that it made his chest tighten.

Sami didn't understand all the politics or the reasons behind the constant violence. He was still a child, too young to grasp the intricacies of borders, treaties, and conflicts that stretched far beyond his small world. But he felt the fear that gripped his parents, the silent tension in his father's eyes whenever he looked at the news, or the way his mother's hands would tremble slightly as she prepared dinner. These things, Sami couldn't fully explain, but he could sense them.

At school, his teacher, Ms. Lina, had tried to give them lessons that would take their minds off the horrors surrounding them. She taught them about history, about the great empires of the world, and the cultures that had shaped human civilization. She taught them about the stars, about the faraway lands that existed beyond the confines of Gaza, about countries that weren't in the grip of war. The subjects brought a sense of escape, a small window through which Sami could look beyond his current reality and dream of a different world, a world where peace was more than just a fleeting wish.

But even at school, Sami could feel the undercurrent of fear. In the eyes of his classmates, in the worried glances exchanged between teachers and students when the noise of artillery rumbled in the distance, in the way some of the boys would laugh too loudly, too nervously, as if trying to pretend that everything was okay. Sami understood that they were trying to find some sense of normalcy, just like he did at home. But it wasn't the same. The tension was palpable, hanging in the air like a thick fog that no one could escape.

Sami's friends would often tell him about the things they had heard, stories of airstrikes, of buildings destroyed, of families torn apart. Sami didn't want to believe them. He couldn't. He didn't want to imagine his world—a world where he had felt so safe and loved—becoming a place of violence and loss.

But it wasn't easy to block out the news. The radio in the corner of the living room, which his father usually turned on in the evening to catch the latest updates, was a constant reminder. Sami didn't like to hear the voices coming from the speakers—the harsh, clipped words that sounded as though they carried more weight than they should. It wasn't the words themselves that terrified him; it was the tone, the urgency, the way it made his parents' faces turn pale, their brows furrowed with worry. Sami couldn't make sense of the words, but he knew the sound of distress when he heard it.

One evening, as the sky began to darken and the orange light from the setting sun filtered through the windows, Sami was playing with Omar in the living room, trying to teach him how to dribble a soccer ball. His mother was in the kitchen, humming softly as she prepared dinner, while Yara was in the corner, studying for her exams. It was a typical evening, quiet and peaceful, yet undercut with a strange, creeping tension.

Then, the sound came.

It was sudden, so loud that Sami's heart seemed to stop for a moment. The walls of their house trembled, and the glass in the windows rattled with a force that made his skin crawl. The distant explosion reverberated through the air, a deep, rumbling sound that seemed to come from the very earth itself. Sami froze. Omar's little face turned pale, and he clutched the soccer ball tightly to his chest, his wide eyes full of confusion.

Layla dropped the knife she had been holding, her hands shaking as she hurried over to Sami and Omar. She pulled them into her arms, her body tense, as if instinctively trying to shield them from something they could not see. Yara looked up from her books, her expression stricken, as she rushed to their side.

"Stay close," Layla whispered, her voice steady but low as if trying to protect them from the very sound of fear in the air.

Sami looked at his father, who had turned pale. Amir was standing by the door, his hand resting on the frame, his eyes distant and troubled. He didn't speak, but the lines of worry deepened on his face. He had seen this before—too many times. He had lived through enough to know what came after the sound of an explosion. Sami could feel it in the way his father stood, his shoulders rigid, his jaw clenched. There was a heaviness in the air that wasn't just about the sound. It was about the realization that, once again, danger was inching closer.

"Papa, what was that?" Sami asked, his voice barely above a whisper.

Amir didn't answer immediately. He closed his eyes for a brief moment as if trying to hold on to the calm before the storm before he finally turned to face his son.

"It's just another warning, Sami," he said, his voice quiet but firm. "Don't worry. Everything will be fine."

But Sami could see the lie in his father's eyes. He wasn't sure what exactly was going on, but he could feel that this time, things felt different. The explosion had sounded too close, too powerful, and the tension in his father's face wasn't something he could easily ignore.

Sami had never known what it was like to live in constant fear. He had heard stories from his friends, yes, but it always felt distant, like something that happened to other people, not to him. Not to his family. But now, as the minutes ticked by and the world outside their house seemed to grow darker, he felt the weight of it.

The air outside became thick with the scent of dust and smoke, the once-clear sky turning hazy and ominous. Sami could hear the distant wail of sirens, the sound of footsteps rushing by as people moved quickly through the streets, as if trying to outrun the inevitable. But no one could escape it—not really.

As the hours passed, the family remained huddled together in the living room, waiting for the all-clear signal that they knew would come eventually.

But the silence between them wasn't comforting. It was heavy, filled with the unspoken understanding that nothing was ever truly safe anymore.

Sami could see his mother trying to maintain her composure, trying to keep things normal for her children. She tried to distract Omar with a story, though her voice quivered slightly, and her hands shook as she held him close. Yara, ever the pragmatic one, had already turned her attention back to her studies, though her eyes kept darting to the window as if she, too, was waiting for something to happen.

It wasn't until later that night, when the lights flickered and then went out completely, that Sami's true fear began to take hold.

Without the soft glow of the lamps or the hum of the refrigerator, the house seemed quieter, and more fragile. The only sounds were the distant explosions, the occasional howl of wind, and the rustling of feet on the floor as his family moved about in the dark. Sami could hear his parents whispering to each other in hushed tones, their words too low for him to catch, but he didn't need to hear them. He knew what they were talking about. They were discussing their plans, making sure they were ready if they had to leave in a hurry.

Sami felt a cold shiver run down his spine. He didn't want to leave. He didn't want to believe that something could happen to them, that the world could turn so dangerous so quickly. But deep down, he knew his parents weren't just talking about the dinner they would eat that night. They were preparing for something much darker.

And as the night wore on, Sami realized that the shadows of conflict were no longer just distant worries. They had crept into his home, settling in with them, making their presence known in the most terrifying way.

Though the explosions had stopped for a moment, Sami knew that peace was never guaranteed here. Peace was a fragile thing, easily shattered, and it was up to them to hold on to it as long as they could. But that night, as Sami lay in bed, staring at the ceiling, he couldn't shake the feeling that something had changed forever.

CHAPTER FIVE

A Glimmer of Hope

The days that followed the rumbling night of explosions seemed to blur into one another. Life in Gaza had always been unpredictable, but since the latest escalation, there was an unsettling sense that nothing could remain unchanged for long. The fear that had settled in the house like an unwelcome guest refused to leave, lurking in every corner, but amidst the unease, there were still moments of light—glimmers of hope that Sami clung to like a child clutching a favorite toy in the dark.

It wasn't always easy to see these glimmers. Some days, the weight of everything—his family's worry, the distant sounds of conflict, the uncertain future—felt like too much to bear. But there were other days when a small event, a brief moment of joy, would remind him of the goodness that still existed in the world.

The day of the school's arts festival was one such moment.

Sami had been excited about the festival for weeks. It wasn't an extravagant event by any means, but it was something to look forward to. There were always so many dreams wrapped up in the event, especially for someone like Sami, who had a deep love for storytelling. The teachers had worked tirelessly with the students to prepare a variety of performances—dramas, songs, and art displays. For Sami, it wasn't about the glitz or glamour of the festival, but rather the chance to share something personal, something that he hoped could make people see the world in a different way.

Weeks before the event, Ms. Lina had announced a writing competition. Sami had entered eagerly, though he wasn't sure if his story was good enough. But Ms. Lina had always been kind, encouraging him to keep writing, to let his imagination run wild. For weeks, Sami had worked on a story—a tale of a magical land where people lived in peace and harmony, a stark contrast to the reality around him. It was a story about the power of hope and how even in the darkest of times, kindness could shine through.

His parents, especially his mother, were so proud of him. They had listened to him read his story over and over at the dinner table, always offering encouragement. Yara, though older and busy with her own studies, would give him playful teasing, telling him he had the potential to be a famous author one day. "If you can dream up a peaceful world in a place like this," she'd told him, "then you've got the power to change things."

The morning of the festival arrived, and there was a sense of quiet excitement in the air. Though the world outside their home was still filled with the tension of conflict, today was about something else. It was a day for the children of Gaza to express themselves, to show that they, too, had dreams—dreams that were bigger than the violence they lived through. Sami's heart raced as he walked to school that morning, holding his story tightly in his hand.

At school, Ms. Lina greeted each student with a warm smile, her presence a source of calm in the chaos of the world outside. The school was a modest building with cracked walls and peeling paint, a remnant of years of neglect, but it had always felt like a sanctuary to Sami. The familiar faces of his friends greeted him as he entered the classroom, each one carrying their own hopes for the day. The atmosphere was electric, with children running around, rehearsing their parts, adjusting their costumes, and finalizing their art projects. Sami could feel the energy building, and for a moment, he forgot about the weight of the world on his shoulders.

The event itself was simple, but it was special. Parents were invited to attend, and the courtyard outside the school was transformed into a temporary stage. Sami's heart pounded as his turn came to present his story. He stepped up to the podium, holding the paper in his hands, and looked out at the audience of teachers, parents, and friends. His eyes scanned the crowd until they landed on his family—his mother, father, and Yara, all seated together, smiling proudly at him. Even Omar, though too young to understand the significance of the event, clapped his hands in excitement.

Sami cleared his throat, feeling a slight nervousness flutter in his chest. But then, he remembered his story, the world he had created in his mind, and the power of words. He took a deep breath and began.

"Once upon a time, there was a land where people lived in peace. They shared everything, from food to love, and they helped one another without question. There were no wars, no fear, and no hunger. The people in this land believed that kindness was stronger than any weapon, and they believed that everyone, no matter where they came from, deserved to live in peace."

Sami paused for a moment, his gaze falling on his family. His mother's eyes were sparkling, her lips slightly parted in admiration, while his father gave him a small, proud nod. Yara's face was full of encouragement, and even Omar was looking up at him with wide eyes, as if he understood the importance of this moment, despite his age.

"The people of this land were not perfect," Sami continued, his voice gaining strength. "They made mistakes, just like everyone does. But when they did, they worked together to fix them. They knew that peace was something that had to be worked for every day, that it wasn't a gift that just fell from the sky. And though they faced challenges, they never gave up on their dream of living together in harmony."

Sami finished the story, his heart racing with the excitement of having shared something so personal. The audience remained quiet for a moment before the applause started, a gentle wave of clapping that rippled through the courtyard. Sami beamed with pride, feeling a warmth in his chest that had nothing to do with the sun beating down on them. For that brief moment, he had transported them all to a place of peace—a place where the world was better than it was.

When he returned to his seat, his family gathered around him, each one offering their congratulations. His mother's arms enveloped him in a tight hug, whispering words of pride and love in his ear. "You were amazing, Sami," she said softly, kissing the top of his head.

Yara was next, ruffling his hair and teasing him with a grin. "That's it, I'm going to start calling you 'the author' from now on," she said.

Even his father, usually the quiet, strong presence in the family, looked at him with a rare, soft expression. "You've got a gift, son," he said. "Don't ever stop telling your stories. They matter."

But it was not just the encouragement from his family that made this moment so special. It was the sense of belonging, of community, that Sami felt. The children of Gaza—his friends and classmates—had all contributed to the festival in their own ways. There was something deeply unifying about their shared effort. The community that had long been bruised by conflict and hardship was coming together, not to fight, but to celebrate their humanity. Even in the face of all the destruction, they had found a way to build something beautiful.

After the event, Sami and his friends played soccer in the schoolyard, kicking the ball around with the same enthusiasm they always did. There was no talk of the world outside, no mention of the bombs or the violence that loomed just beyond the school gates. For a brief moment, the joy of being a child, of laughing and playing with friends, washed away the weight of reality.

When Sami returned home that evening, he couldn't help but feel lighter. His family gathered for dinner, and despite the persistent fear that lurked in the corners of their lives, there was a sense of peace at the table. They ate together, talking about the festival, joking and laughing like they hadn't in weeks.

As the evening drew to a close, Sami felt something he hadn't felt in a long time—a quiet sense of hope. He didn't know what tomorrow would bring. He didn't know if the conflict would escalate again, or if they would have to face another night of fear and uncertainty. But for tonight, he had created something that was all his own. His words, his dreams, his story—they had a power all their own, one that no bomb or conflict could take away.

In the days that followed, Sami wrote more stories—stories of peace, of love, of hope. Each time he sat down with a pen in his hand, he was reminded that even in a world so torn by conflict, the power of imagination could still build something beautiful.

And as long as he held on to that, he believed, there would always be a glimmer of hope.

CHAPTER SIX

THE STORM BEGINS

It had been weeks since Sami felt the shift. The usual hum of life in Gaza—punctuated by its everyday struggles and fleeting joys—had changed. The air felt heavier, the world more tense. He could see it in his mother's eyes, the way she would glance at the clock nervously or whisper to his father when she thought Sami wasn't listening. He could feel it in the air around their home, where the echoes of explosions grew louder and closer with each passing day. The sounds that used to be distant, muted by the walls of their home, were now sharp and jarring, shaking the very ground beneath them. Sami tried to tell himself that it was just another phase—another temporary conflict that would soon pass, as they always did—but something told him this time was different.

The days were long, stretching on like an unyielding road that seemed to have no end. The mornings still began with the sun breaking through the thin curtains in Sami's room, casting its golden light on the walls. It was always quiet in the early hours, the city still asleep before the bustle of life began. Sami would wake up, stretch his arms wide, and run to his window, peering outside to catch a glimpse of the world before it awoke in full force. But recently, that world had felt more fragile. His neighborhood, once alive with the sounds of children playing in the streets, now seemed quieter, more distant.

It wasn't that the children were no longer playing. No, they still ran through the streets, kicking soccer balls, laughing, and trying to forget the uncertainty of their world. But there was something different in the air. A silence hung around them like a veil—heavy, oppressive, like a storm waiting to break.

Sami's mother had become more vigilant in recent days, her concern growing as the conflict neared their neighborhood. She had always been the steady presence in their lives, a calm force amid the chaos. But now, Sami could see her eyes darting nervously as she moved around the house. She checked the windows more frequently, making sure they were secure, and often paused by the door, listening for any sound of approaching danger. There were whispers among the adults—rumors of airstrikes, warnings of increased tensions. Sami didn't fully understand it, but he could sense the fear. The unspoken anxiety that seemed to settle over everything.

Yara, too, had noticed the change. The evening dinners, once filled with lighthearted teasing and playful banter, had become quieter. They ate with less conversation, and Yara's smile—usually so bright and warm—was now tinged with concern. It wasn't just the conflict; it was the uncertainty. The not knowing when the next escalation would happen, or where the next bomb might fall. Yara had always been the practical one, focused on her studies and future, her dream of becoming a doctor anchoring her in a world that often felt like it was spiraling out of control. But now, she, too, seemed distracted, her eyes often lingering on the window as if she were waiting for something, anything, to happen.

Sami's father, the quiet strength of their family, had always been the one to reassure them. His calm voice and steady hands had always been a source of comfort, especially when the air felt thick with tension. But even he had begun to show signs of strain. There was an unease in the way he moved around the house, the way he lingered by the door at night, listening for sounds in the distance. He had been preparing them for months—teaching Sami and Yara how to react in case of an emergency, how to stay calm, and how to make sure they could get to safety quickly. It had been a drill, something that Sami had once thought of as little more than an exercise. But now, it felt more real, more urgent. It wasn't just a drill anymore.

The nights had become the hardest. Sami couldn't remember when the sounds of explosions had first started, but he knew they were growing closer. Each night, as the darkness settled over Gaza, it seemed as though the very air around them was charged with a kind of quiet anticipation, the calm before a storm. Sometimes it was a distant rumble, the low roar of something far off. Other times, it was a sharp crack of thunder, the sound of a bomb, far too close for comfort.

One evening, as Sami lay in bed, his mind racing with thoughts of the day's events, the unmistakable sound of an explosion shattered the silence. It was close—closer than any blast he had ever heard before. Sami sat up in bed, his heart pounding in his chest. He could hear the familiar sound of his parents moving in the next room, their voices low and urgent. His father was speaking quickly, and calmly, urging them to stay quiet, to stay alert. Sami could hear his mother's voice, trembling slightly as she reassured his younger brother, Omar, who had begun to cry.

In that moment, the fear in the air seemed palpable, like a physical presence. Sami's fingers tightened around the sheets as he tried to calm his racing thoughts. What was happening? Why was it getting so much worse?

"Stay close to us, Sami," his father's voice called out from the hallway. His tone was steady, but there was something there—a tightness, a layer of fear that Sami had never heard before.

Sami quickly got out of bed and rushed to the hallway. His father was standing at the door, Yara beside him, holding Omar close. His mother was gathering a few things—blankets, water bottles, anything that might be needed if they had to leave in a hurry. The urgency in their movements was unsettling. They had done this before, practiced for this moment. But now, with the threat no longer just a distant possibility, it felt real. Too real.

Sami's father turned to him, his eyes soft but firm. "Get your shoes on," he said. "We're going to the safe place, just like we practiced."

Sami nodded, though his heart was in his throat. He had always imagined these drills as nothing more than preparation. But now, as the sounds of explosions continued to echo through the night, he knew there was no pretending anymore. This was real.

Within moments, they had gathered their things and moved quickly through the house. The air was thick with the sounds of chaos, the distant hum of sirens, and the sharp crack of explosions. Sami's hand gripped his father's, and he could feel the tension in his palm, the fear that his father was trying so hard to keep hidden. Yara held Omar tightly, her face pale, her eyes wide with worry. She whispered soothing words to him, but Sami could see the fear in her own eyes.

They moved swiftly through the narrow streets of their neighborhood, the familiar sights around them now foreign, transformed by the urgency of the moment. The streetlights flickered overhead, casting eerie shadows on the cracked pavement. The usual buzz of life had vanished, replaced by the sounds of hurried footsteps, the occasional shout, and the distant echoes of airstrikes.

It felt like a nightmare.

As they reached the small underground shelter near the end of the street, a sense of cold dread settled over Sami. He had been there before, during drills, when everything had been calm when it had felt like a game. But now, with the bombs falling in the distance and the tension thick in the air, the shelter seemed too small, too suffocating. He could feel the walls closing in as they gathered inside, huddling together in the dim light.

Sami could hear his family's breathing, each of them trying to calm the others, but it was clear to him that they were all scared. His mother held Omar tightly, whispering comforting words to him, even though her voice trembled. Yara sat close to Sami, her hand on his shoulder, her eyes darting to the entrance as though waiting for something to happen.

Sami tried to stay calm, but his mind kept racing. He thought about his school, his friends, the soccer games they played, and the stories he had written. It all felt so distant now, like a dream that he might never wake up from. The world outside was changing, and there was nothing he could do to stop it.

The storm had begun.

Outside, the world was unraveling. The bombs fell, the ground shook, and everything that had once felt certain—his family, his neighborhood, his life—was now suspended in a state of constant, terrifying uncertainty. Sami didn't know what would happen next. He didn't know if he would see his home again, or if the world would ever feel safe again. But in that moment, as they huddled together in the darkness, he felt one thing clearly: fear. Fear, but also the undeniable sense that they had to hold on. Hold on to each other, to the little things, to the hope that tomorrow might bring something better.

And so, with his family by his side, Sami closed his eyes and held his breath, waiting for the storm to pass.

CHAPTER SEVEN

THE NIGHT OF LOSS

It was the kind of night that crept up on you slowly, like the tightening grip of a storm, heavy and suffocating. The dark sky outside their shelter was pregnant with the promise of something terrible, the air still with tension so thick, it felt as if the earth itself was holding its breath. Sami lay on the cold, damp floor of the shelter, his small body curled up beside his mother, his father's strong hand on his shoulder. He could hear his own heartbeat pulsing in his ears, the sound mingling with the distant echoes of explosions, a constant reminder that they were living through something unthinkable.

They had been in the shelter for hours, perhaps more, though Sami had long since lost track of time. The air smelled of dust, stale sweat, and the faint metallic tang of fear. Every now and then, he would hear the distant hum of aircraft, the deep rumble of explosions, followed by the eerie silence that always came afterward. It was a silence that spoke volumes—of destruction, of loss, of lives turned upside down.

Sami clung to his mother's side, her arm wrapped protectively around him, her warmth a small comfort against the fear that clawed at his chest. His father sat beside them, trying to keep the atmosphere calm, but Sami could sense the unease in his every movement. His father's normally steady hands trembled ever so slightly as he checked the small emergency radio they had brought along, his eyes narrowing as he listened to the crackling static. Yara sat next to them, holding Omar close, her face pale, her eyes wide with the same quiet terror that had taken over everyone in the shelter.

Everything felt wrong.

Sami had never been afraid like this before. As a child, he had always been protected by his family's love and their unwavering belief that everything would be okay, and that things would always work out. But tonight, in this suffocating darkness, with the world outside crumbling, he realized how fragile that sense of safety had always been. The war had come to their doorstep, and it wasn't leaving.

"Stay close, Sami," his mother whispered, her voice soft but trembling. "We're here. We're together. Everything will be okay."

But Sami knew better. The words felt empty, and hollow, like promises whispered in a storm that was too fierce to be calmed by mere words. He nodded, but even as he did, a sick feeling curled in his stomach, a sense of dread that seemed to come from deep within, from a place he couldn't name. He wanted to believe her, wanted to feel the comfort of her embrace the way he had so many times before. But tonight, it felt like nothing would ever be the same again.

Then came the noise.

It was like the entire world had just exploded in one deafening, bone-shaking roar. The ground trembled beneath them, a violent quake that sent a jolt of terror through Sami's body. He heard the crash of something—glass, metal, stone—shattering all at once, followed by the sickening sound of concrete splintering apart. His ears rang with the intensity of the blast, the reverberations of the shockwave traveling through the walls of their small shelter like a living thing, clawing its way into their bones. It was as if the earth itself had been ripped open.

Sami's heart stopped, his breath caught in his throat. His father yelled for them to stay down, but the words were drowned out by the terrible noise. Sami's mother's grip tightened around him, but even her strength couldn't quell the terror that surged through him. They were trapped. The world outside had exploded, and there was nowhere to run.

Everything blurred in an instant. Sami felt as if time had stretched out and then snapped back, a rubber band pulled too tightly and let go. The air seemed to crackle with the heat of destruction, and his entire body felt weightless as if he were floating as if the world had lifted him off the ground. But the moment was fleeting—too fleeting—before everything crashed down upon him with the force of a thousand storms.

And then, there was nothing.

The world went silent.

Sami blinked, disoriented, his mind struggling to piece together what had just happened. For a moment, he thought perhaps he had lost his hearing, the blast's aftereffects still ringing in his head. But then he realized that the silence wasn't just in his ears—it was in the very air around them as if the world had exhaled, holding its breath, waiting.

Sami sat up, his chest tight with panic, his thoughts racing as he tried to make sense of the chaos. The shelter around them had grown impossibly still, the dark space now suffused with an eerie quiet that made his skin crawl. His eyes searched the dimness, trying to find something—anything—to hold on to. His heart pounded in his chest as he tried to breathe through the rising panic.

"Mom?" His voice cracked as he called out, the word echoing in the stillness. His throat felt tight like he was suffocating on his own fear.

No response.

"Dad? Yara?" His voice grew more frantic as he scrambled to his feet. His eyes darted around the shelter, searching the shadows for his family. But all he saw was the dim outline of the walls, the debris scattered around the floor. His parents—his sister—where were they?

Sami's breath came in shallow gasps, his mind struggling to understand the impossible. The shelter had been sturdy, built to withstand the worst that Gaza had to offer. But now it felt fragile, like paper in the wind, like it could collapse with the slightest touch. He felt as though the ground beneath him might crumble at any moment, taking him with it.

His feet moved instinctively, carrying him toward the entrance of the shelter. He tried to call out again, his voice weak and desperate, but no words came. Only the gnawing panic, the fear of what he might find. The silence pressed in around him, thick and suffocating.

He reached the door, his hand trembling as he pushed it open.

What he saw outside was a nightmare he couldn't have imagined.

The street was barely recognizable. What had once been their neighborhood, the place where they had laughed, played, and lived, was now a battlefield, reduced to rubble. The ground was scarred with craters, and the buildings that had once lined the streets were now reduced to twisted heaps of metal and shattered concrete. The air was thick with dust and smoke, and the sky above them was choked with the remnants of the explosion. The faint smell of burning wood and metal filled his nostrils, the acrid scent of something lost, something gone forever.

And then he heard it—a faint sound, like the distant cry of a child. His heart leaped in his chest, the hope surging within him like a lifeline. It was his family. It had to be. They had to be alive.

He stumbled toward the sound, his legs shaking beneath him, his eyes wild with fear. His mind was a blur, each step more desperate than the last, each breath coming harder as he pushed forward into the destruction. The smoke and dust made it difficult to see, but he refused to stop, refused to believe that they were gone.

He called out again, his voice raw, cracked with emotion. "Mom! Dad! Yara! Omar!"

The sound of his own voice felt foreign to him, the words heavy with grief, with terror. But no answer came. Only the wind, carrying the remnants of destruction, the faint echo of a world torn apart.

And then he saw it.

A piece of something—his mother's scarf—fluttering in the wind, caught on a jagged piece of rubble. Sami's breath caught in his throat. He rushed forward, his hands trembling as he reached out to touch it, to pull it from the wreckage. The fabric was soft and familiar. But as his fingers brushed it, his heart sank. Beneath the debris, there was nobody. No sign of his family.

"Mom?" he whispered, his voice barely audible, the word barely a breath. The sound was swallowed by the wind, lost in the vast, empty silence that had taken over their world.

Tears began to sting his eyes as his heart shattered into a thousand pieces. No. No, no, no. This couldn't be happening. This wasn't real.

But the truth began to settle in his chest, cold and unforgiving. His family—his mother, father, Yara, Omar—they were gone. The blast had taken them. It had taken everything.

Sami fell to his knees, his body trembling with the force of his grief. He had never felt so alone, so empty. The pain was a jagged knife, slicing through him with each breath. He didn't know how to process it, how to bear the weight of the world now crushing him.

He had lost them.

And in that moment, the world around him, once filled with life and love, was nothing but ruins. He was alone in the darkness, with only his memories to hold on to.

And even those, it seemed, were slipping away.

CHAPTER EIGHT

ALONE IN THE RUINS

Sami awoke to the sharp scent of antiseptic and the faint hum of machines, a strange and unfamiliar sound that made him flinch, his heart skipping a beat. His eyes fluttered open, the light too bright and too harsh after the dark, suffocating night. For a moment, he couldn't understand where he was. His head felt heavy, his body sore, as if it had been pulled through a thousand years of pain. He blinked, trying to focus, but everything seemed distant, blurry, as though he were looking through the wrong end of a telescope.

His mind reeled, disoriented, trying to make sense of the foreign surroundings. The walls around him were white, sterile, and cold. He was lying in a bed, not the floor of his home, not the safety of his mother's embrace. Panic surged through him like a tide, his heart hammering in his chest. His hands trembled as he tried to sit up, only to be greeted with a sharp pain in his side. He winced, the pressure in his ribs too much, and he lay back down, gasping for breath.

The quiet, too quiet, of the hospital room, suffocated him. There was no sound of his father's steady voice or Yara's gentle teasing. No laughter from Omar, no rustle of his mother's clothes as she moved about. It was just silence—the kind of silence that gnawed at his soul, digging deeper with every passing second.

"Mom?" he whispered, his voice hoarse and raw, as if it hadn't been used in days. "Dad? Yara?"

No answer came, and the emptiness grew inside him, swallowing him whole.

His eyes scanned the room frantically. There were others here—strangers—who moved quietly through the space, their faces tired, their eyes haunted. But no one was looking at him. No one cared about Sami, the little boy who had lost everything, the boy whose world had been ripped apart in a single night. There was no one left to care.

He was alone.

The thought hit him like a punch to the gut, knocking the air from his lungs, the realization almost more than he could bear. His family—his mother, father, Yara, Omar—they were gone. The blast, the explosion that had torn through their world, had taken them all. They hadn't made it. He had woken up, but they hadn't. They hadn't been lucky enough to survive.

Tears welled in his eyes, but he refused to let them fall. He clenched his fists at his sides, the pain in his chest growing with each labored breath. He couldn't—he couldn't cry. He couldn't afford to break. Not yet. Not here, not now. But it was as though the dam inside him had cracked, and the flood of emotions surged through him, pushing against every part of him that tried to hold it all together.

How was he supposed to survive without them? How was he supposed to go on?

Sami turned his head toward the window, hoping to find some sense of familiarity, some sense of normalcy, but all he saw was more devastation. The once familiar skyline of Gaza, with its bustling streets, and its people laughing and living, was now a broken, crumbling wreck. He could see the aftermath of the night—the shattered buildings, the jagged edges of collapsed homes, the lifeless streets. Everything was in ruins. And it was all his fault.

It wasn't supposed to be like this.

He had promised his mother that everything would be okay, that they would be fine. He had promised Yara he would take care of Omar, and that he would always protect them. He had promised his father that he would be strong, that he would be the man of the house when his father could no longer carry the weight. But all of those promises felt empty now.

Who was he without them?

"Why didn't I stay with them?" Sami whispered to no one, his voice trembling with guilt. "Why didn't I... I should have stayed. I should have stayed with them!"

He closed his eyes, trying to block out the vision of their faces, trying to block out the image of his mother's tender smile, his father's warm embrace, and Yara's laughter ringing through the house. They were gone. They had vanished in an instant, taken by the explosion that Sami could still hear in his mind. The roar of it, the earth-shaking power of it, had felt like the world was ending like nothing would ever be the same again. And in a way, nothing ever would be.

The door to the room opened slowly, and Sami's eyes shot up, his heart pounding. A figure stood in the doorway—a man, not much older than Sami's father had been, wearing the simple clothes of a volunteer. His face was kind, his eyes gentle, but there was a weariness in his gaze, a sadness that reflected the world around them. He held a small tray in his hands, a few cups of water, and what looked like some bread.

"Sami?" the man asked softly, his voice almost too soft. "How are you feeling?"

Sami didn't answer. He couldn't find the words. He didn't want to say anything. He didn't want to talk to anyone. What was the point? His family was gone, and nothing else mattered. He didn't matter anymore.

The man seemed to sense this. He set the tray down on a small table beside the bed, taking a cautious step closer to Sami. "I know this is hard," he said gently, his voice full of quiet understanding. "But you're not alone, okay? There are people who want to help you. We're here for you."

Sami stared at him, his heart hardening. No one could help him. No one could fix this. His mother had always told him that help was something you found when you needed it most, but the truth was, he didn't need help. He needed his family. He needed to go home.

"Who are you?" Sami asked bitterly, his voice sharp despite the tears that still threatened to fall. "What can you do? My family's gone. There's nothing left for me."

The volunteer didn't flinch, didn't retreat in the face of Sami's anger. Instead, he sat down beside the bed, his gaze never leaving the boy. "I understand you're hurting, Sami," he said softly. "But you're still here. And that means something. You have a life to live, even without them. You're not alone. Not anymore."

Sami looked at him, his chest tight with a mix of emotions. He wanted to scream, to lash out at this stranger who couldn't possibly understand. How could he? He didn't know what it felt like to lose everything, to lose the people who meant the world to you.

"I don't want to live without them," Sami muttered, his voice barely a whisper. "I want to go back to them. I want to be with them."

The volunteer's face softened, and he placed a hand gently on Sami's arm. "I know it feels impossible right now," he said quietly. "And it's okay to feel lost, to feel angry and sad. But there's still hope, Sami. Your family—they loved you. They would want you to live, to keep going. They wouldn't want you to give up."

Sami swallowed hard, his throat tight with unshed tears. "How do you know that?" he whispered, almost accusingly. "How do you know what they would want?"

The volunteer didn't answer right away. Instead, he took a deep breath, as if carefully choosing his next words. "Because I've seen this before," he said quietly. "I've seen children like you—children who have lost everything. And I've seen them find a way to keep going. It's not easy, and it's not quick. But it's possible. And you don't have to do it alone."

Sami closed his eyes, his mind spinning. The words didn't make sense to him, not in the way he needed them to. His grief was a gaping wound, raw and aching, and there was nothing anyone could do to heal it. But there was something about the volunteer's voice—something in the way he spoke, something in the quiet hope in his eyes—that made Sami wonder if there might be a way forward.

Not right now. Not today. But maybe, someday.

"Why are you helping me?" Sami asked, his voice breaking as he looked up at the man.

The volunteer smiled gently. "Because you're important. And because there are people who care about you. Even if it doesn't feel like it right now, you matter. You always will."

Sami didn't know what to say to that. He felt the weight of the world pressing down on him, suffocating him. But for the first time since waking up, there was a flicker of something deep inside—a tiny spark of something that resembled hope. It was fragile, but it was there.

And that, perhaps, was the first step toward finding a way forward.

CHAPTER NINE

REBUILDING A BROKEN SPIRIT

The days in the hospital blurred together, like pages of a book torn from their bindings, scattered and tossed to the winds. Sami had no sense of time. There was no way to track the passing of the hours or the days. He awoke each morning in the sterile white room, the same harsh lights above him, the same cold metal bed beneath him. His body felt foreign, bruised, and tired, but his heart was the heaviest of all. His spirit was cracked, shattered beyond recognition, and nothing seemed capable of mending it. His family, his world—gone in an instant—and there was nothing, no one, to fill the hollow void they had left.

Sami barely ate. He barely spoke. He lay in bed for hours, staring at the ceiling, his eyes unfocused, lost in memories he couldn't hold onto. The sounds of the hospital—the beeping of machines, the hushed voices of nurses and doctors moving through the halls—felt like noise he couldn't escape. It reminded him that the world kept turning, that life kept moving forward, while his own had been frozen in time, locked in that moment of horror, the moment when his family had been ripped from him.

The pain was suffocating. It was a tight knot in his chest that never loosened, a heavyweight that dragged him down. Every time he closed his eyes, he saw them—his mother, her face warm and loving as she tucked him into bed; his father, strong and steady, always there with a reassuring smile; Yara, always looking out for him, teasing him, laughing with him; Omar, his baby brother, who had depended on him for everything. He saw them, but they were fading, their faces blurry, their voices softening. And in those moments, Sami could hardly breathe.

He couldn't imagine a world without them, and yet, this was his new reality. A reality where their absence felt like a physical pain, sharp and jagged, a wound that could never heal.

It was in this suffocating silence, in this black hole of grief, that Nabil found him again.

Nabil had been a constant presence in the hospital since the explosion. He was a volunteer—one of the many who had come in the aftermath to help, to offer comfort to those who had lost everything. Sami had barely noticed him at first. His world had been too small, too filled with darkness and loss to care about the kindness of strangers. But Nabil had remained patient, always there, never pushing too hard, simply waiting for Sami to acknowledge him.

One afternoon, after what felt like an eternity of staring at the blank walls of his hospital room, Sami heard footsteps approaching. It wasn't the usual shuffle of nurses, nor the hurried pace of a doctor. These footsteps were slower, more deliberate. Sami's eyes flickered toward the door, and there, standing in the doorway, was Nabil.

The volunteer smiled gently at him, though his eyes carried the weight of their shared grief. There was something in his gaze that spoke of a sadness Sami couldn't fully understand but somehow recognized. It was a sadness that lingered, that never truly left, but also one that had learned to live alongside the pain.

"Sami," Nabil said, his voice soft but steady. "How are you feeling today?"

Sami didn't answer. He couldn't answer. Words felt useless now, like trying to capture a fleeting shadow. He simply stared at Nabil, feeling a strange pull in his chest. The man had been kind to him, offering small acts of comfort that, at the time, had felt insignificant. But now, as Sami sat in his isolation, the warmth of that kindness was the only thing that didn't make him feel invisible.

Nabil sat down beside the bed, his presence quiet but steady. He didn't ask Sami to talk, didn't press him to explain the thoughts swirling inside his head. Instead, he simply sat there, his gaze soft, his hand resting lightly on the arm of the chair. He let the silence stretch between them, an unspoken understanding passing through the air.

After what felt like an eternity of silence, Nabil spoke again. "I know you're hurting, Sami. I know it feels like the pain will never go away. But I need you to understand something: it's okay to hurt. It's okay to grieve. But you can't let that grief consume you. You have a choice. You can let it break you, or you can let it make you stronger. It's your choice."

Sami's heart clenched at the words. He didn't want to hear them. He didn't want anyone telling him what he should or shouldn't do. He wanted to scream, to rage against the unfairness of it all, to shout at the world for taking his family away from him. He wanted to close his eyes and never open them again, to fall into the darkness and forget everything.

But as much as he hated to admit it, something in Nabil's words made sense. The weight of his grief had been suffocating him, dragging him down into a pit of despair. And as much as he wanted to remain there, to stay in the quiet, familiar pain, there was a part of him—a small, flickering part—that wanted to fight. That wanted to find a way out.

Nabil didn't push him, but his presence was a quiet reminder that there was a life beyond the hospital room. That there was something worth fighting for, even in the midst of all the pain. And though Sami wasn't ready to face that reality yet, he couldn't deny the flicker of hope that had started to grow in his chest.

"Your family loved you, Sami," Nabil continued, his voice steady but filled with empathy. "They wanted the best for you. They would want you to live, to keep going. And I know that might not make sense right now, but the truth is, they live on in you. In the way you remember them, in the way you keep their love alive."

Sami's chest tightened, his breath catching in his throat. He hadn't realized how badly he needed to hear those words, how much he had been longing for someone to tell him that it was okay to keep living. That it was okay to honor his family by continuing to breathe, to move, to find a way forward. It felt impossible, but in that moment, it didn't feel quite as impossible as it had before.

"How do I move forward?" Sami whispered, his voice breaking. "How do I keep going without them?"

Nabil smiled, though there was sadness in his eyes. "One step at a time, Sami. One day at a time. You don't have to have all the answers right now. You don't have to know what the future holds. But you do have a choice. You can choose to let your grief define you, or you can choose to honor the love your family gave you by living in their memory."

The words sank deep into Sami's heart, and for the first time since the explosion, something inside him shifted. He didn't know how to take that first step, didn't know how to leave the pain behind. But he knew that he couldn't stay in this hospital room forever, couldn't live in the shadows of his grief for the rest of his life. His family had given him so much—love, laughter, support—and he couldn't throw all of that away.

"I don't know if I can do it," Sami admitted, his voice quiet, uncertain. "I don't know if I can live without them."

"You don't have to do it alone," Nabil replied softly. "You have people who care about you. And you have yourself. You're stronger than you think."

Sami didn't know if he believed Nabil's words. He didn't know if he was strong enough to face the future without his family by his side. But as he looked at Nabil, as he saw the quiet encouragement in his eyes, he felt a flicker of something deep inside. A small, fragile hope that maybe—just maybe—there was a way forward. That, one day, he would find the strength to live, not just for himself, but for the memory of his family.

In the days that followed, Sami began to find small moments of peace. He started to engage with Nabil more, answering his questions, and listening to his stories. He didn't speak much about his family—not yet—but Nabil didn't force him. Slowly, Sami began to remember the things that had made his family so special—the way his mother had hummed softly as she prepared their meals, the way his father had always been there to fix things when they broke, the way Yara had laughed so freely as if the world was a bright and beautiful place.

In those quiet moments of remembering, Sami realized that his family hadn't truly left him. Their love still lived within him, in every memory, in every quiet smile he shared with Nabil. And even though the road ahead would be long and difficult, it was no longer a road he had to walk alone.

The healing had only just begun, but Sami was ready to take that first step.

CHAPTER TEN

A NEW PATH FORWARD

The light of the early morning poured through the cracked window of Sami's small room, casting long shadows across the floor. The rays fell gently on his face as he lay in the bed, still and quiet, his eyes barely open. The soft warmth was a reminder that, despite the coldness of the world around him, the sun still rose. The earth still turned. Life, it seemed, continued even in the face of all the pain.

Sami had always been a dreamer. When he was younger, he had dreamed of becoming a soccer player, of running down wide fields with the wind in his hair and the crowd cheering his name. But as he lay there, staring at the ceiling, he realized that those dreams had changed. They had shifted in the most profound way, becoming something deeper, more meaningful.

Sami had always loved stories. His mother had been the first to teach him the magic of words, reading him tales of faraway lands and heroic figures. His father had always been a storyteller, too, weaving stories of his own childhood, of a world long passed but filled with hope and adventure. Yara, his sister, had been an artist at heart, drawing pictures to go along with the stories they told. Together, they had created a world of dreams—a world filled with laughter, love, and endless possibilities.

Now, in the silence of his room, Sami understood what he had to do. He had to keep telling those stories. Not just the stories of the past, not just the stories of his family, but stories that could help others understand the pain he had endured. Stories that could show the world the beauty of hope and resilience, even in the darkest of times.

Sami had always been surrounded by stories, but now it was his turn to tell them. He could no longer allow the weight of his grief to hold him down. He could no longer hide from the pain, thinking that somehow it would pass on its own. His mother had always told him that "hope is like a seed—you plant it, and you watch it grow." It was time to plant that seed.

As he sat up in bed, a feeling of determination washed over him. The numbness, the suffocating darkness, was still there, but it didn't have the same grip it once did. The memories of his family were now more than just sources of pain. They were pieces of him, pieces of the person he was meant to become. His mother's nurturing warmth, his father's wisdom, and quiet strength, Yara's laughter, Omar's innocence—they were all a part of him now. They had not left him. They lived within him, in the very core of his being.

The thought of them filled him with a bittersweet ache, but also with a fierce sense of purpose. He would carry their love with him wherever he went. They had given him everything they could, and now it was up to him to honor that legacy. He couldn't let their lives—his family's lives—be reduced to tragedy. They deserved better than that.

Sami stood slowly, his legs shaky but determined. He had learned to walk again, not just physically, but emotionally. The journey ahead would not be easy. There would be more nights filled with tears, more days when the grief would return like a storm cloud threatening to break. But Sami had begun to understand something profound: grief didn't erase love. It didn't erase memories. And it certainly didn't erase hope.

Hope was what had kept him going through the darkest moments. Hope was what had kept him alive when all he wanted to do was disappear. He could feel it now, like a flicker in his chest, a quiet flame that refused to go out. He couldn't see the whole path ahead of him, but he could see the next step. And that was enough for now.

Sami began to write. The words came slowly at first as if they were hesitant, unsure of themselves. He started with small details, the little things he remembered so clearly about his family: the way his mother's laugh had sounded when she found something funny, the way his father's eyes would crinkle when he smiled, the way Yara always made him feel safe. These were the pieces of his life, the building blocks of a future he was determined to create.

But the words grew faster. They grew stronger. As he wrote, he began to realize something he hadn't fully understood before: his story wasn't just his own. It was everyone's story. The story of loss, of survival, of resilience. The story of a child who had lost everything but had found the strength to live. Sami wasn't alone in his grief. He wasn't alone in his pain. There were millions of others like him, children and adults alike, who had been torn from their homes, from their families, from their futures. He wanted to speak for them, to tell their stories, to give them the voice that had been taken from them.

The words on the page became his way of reaching out, of connecting with the world. They became his way of remembering his family, of keeping their legacy alive. He would write about the love they had shared, about the dreams they had built together, about the world they had lost. But he would also write about the hope that could rise from the ashes. He would write about the possibility of a future where no more children would have to endure the same pain he had. He would write about the strength that lay within the human spirit to rebuild, to rise from the wreckage, and to create something beautiful, even when everything seemed broken.

Days turned into weeks, and weeks turned into months. Sami's writing became a lifeline, a way for him to process the grief, to give it shape and meaning. He shared his stories with Nabil, who encouraged him to keep going, to not give up. Nabil had become more than just a volunteer to Sami. He had become a mentor, a guide who showed him that healing was possible, even when it seemed impossible.

But there were still moments when Sami doubted himself when the grief felt too heavy to bear. There were nights when he would sit by the window, staring out into the darkness, feeling the weight of his memories pressing down on him. He would think of his family, of all they had been, of all they had lost. And in those moments, it felt as though nothing would ever fill the emptiness inside him.

But then he would remember something his father had told him long ago: "In the darkest times, look for the light. It may be small, but it is always there."

And Sami would hold onto that. The light. The hope. The belief that, no matter how broken the world seemed, there was always a way forward. There was always a reason to keep going.

One day, Sami's stories were noticed. A local journalist, who had been working with Nabil and the other volunteers, heard about Sami's writing. The journalist reached out to him, asking if he would share his story with the world. At first, Sami hesitated. He wasn't sure he was ready to expose his pain, to share the rawness of his grief with others. But then he thought of his family, of the love they had given him, and of the hope they had instilled in him. He thought of all the children who had lost their families, who had been torn from their homes, and who were now living with the same pain he had.

Sami agreed. His story was published, and it spread far beyond the small town where he lived. People from all over the world read his words, felt his pain, and were inspired by his strength. His story became a beacon of hope, a reminder that even in the darkest of times, there was always the possibility of healing, of rebuilding, and of creating a future that honored those who had come before.

Sami never forgot his family. Their memory was always with him, like a soft whisper in his heart. But he also understood that life was still waiting for him. He had a future to build, a life to live, and a world to change. He had a voice now, and he would use it. He would write, he would speak, and he would never stop sharing his story, no matter how difficult it might be.

For the first time since the explosion, Sami felt a sense of peace. It wasn't the absence of pain, but the presence of something deeper—a purpose, a reason to keep going. And in that quiet peace, he knew he was not alone. His family was with him, their love still shining bright. And he would carry that light with him, always, as he walked the path ahead.

Sami took a deep breath and looked out the window. The sun was setting, and the sky was painted in hues of orange and pink. The world was still there, still turning. And for the first time in a long while, Sami was ready to face it.

There was still so much to do, so much to learn. But he had hope now. And that was enough.

The light had found its way back into his heart. And he knew, without a doubt, that he would keep moving forward, one step at a time.

* * * THE END * * *